Using This Unit

The activities in *Reading to Follow Instructions* can be used in several ways.

- You may present lessons in the order they occur in the book.
- You may choose to present each section as a need arises in your classroom.
- You many determine that students need only certain of the sections.

Some classes will need to do all of the practice activities with teacher guidance before moving on to the independent activities. Other classes will need only a review before beginning the small group and independents tasks.

Although sample materials are provided for each topic covered in this unit, the best places to practice reading to follow instructions will come from actual class and home experiences.

Classroom Environment

Surround your students with opportunities to read and follow instructions:
- Place charts with instructions at centers and other work areas.
- Hang charts of class rules and responsibilities.
- Put instructions for assignments on the chalkboard or instruction sheets.
- Provide various types of board and card games with written instructions.
- Provide a section in your class library of books containing art, craft, and science projects appropriate for your students.
- Prepare additional lessons of your own following the lesson formats in this unit.

Prepare Assessment Checklist

Reproduce the reading assessment checklist on page 3. Keep the checklist in a binder and use to:

- check specific reading behaviors observed.
- note special problems.
- plan individual or small group lessons in areas of need.

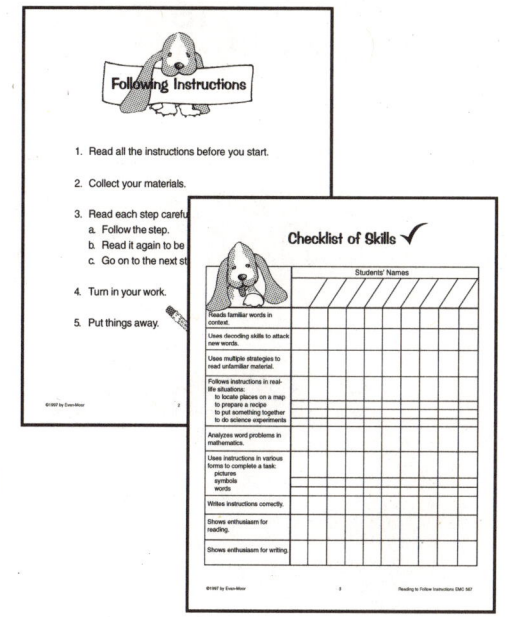

Following Instructions Chart

Prepare a chart of steps for following instructions. Write the instructions on a sheet of chart paper or enlarge page 2 and mount it on tagboard.

Centers

Create a set of center activities. Place each center's materials and instructions in a container (folder, envelope, box, can, etc.). Pages 50 - 64 contain instructions for six centers. Develop more centers as they are needed. Choose instructions and projects that support your specific curriculum.

Following Instructions

1. Read all the instructions before you start.

2. Collect your materials.

3. Read each step carefully.
    a. Follow the step.
    b. Read it again to be sure you did everything.
    c. Go on to the next step.

4. Turn in your work.

5. Put things away.

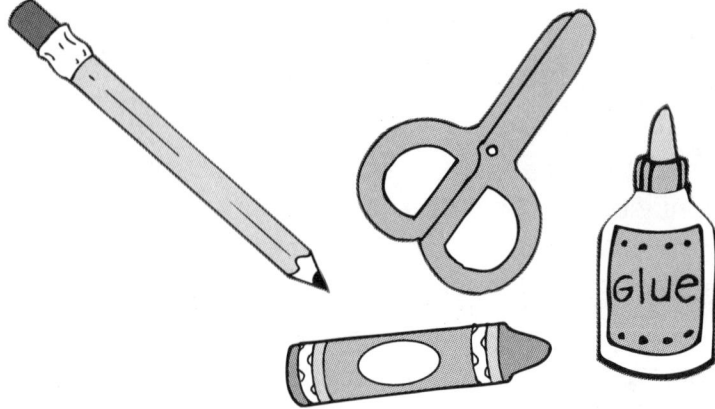

Checklist of Skills ✓

	Students' Names								
Reads familiar words in context.									
Uses decoding skills to attack new words.									
Uses multiple strategies to read unfamiliar material.									
Follows instructions in real-life situations:									
to locate places on a map									
to prepare a recipe									
to put something together									
to do science experiments									
Analyzes word problems in mathematics.									
Uses instructions in various forms to complete a task:									
pictures									
symbols									
words									
Writes instructions correctly.									
Shows enthusiasm for reading.									
Shows enthusiasm for writing.									

©1997 by Evan-Moor   Reading to Follow Instructions EMC 567

An Introduction

Introduce the concept of "following instructions" using some or all of these activities. You will begin with students listening to oral instructions and then do similar activities following written instructions.

Discussion

Discuss the concept of "instructions" with your students. Guide the discussion with questions such as these:

"When do we use them?"
"Why are they important?"
"What makes instructions good/useful?"
"Why is it important to read/listen carefully?"

Brainstorm with students to list all the times they have had to follow oral or written instructions today.

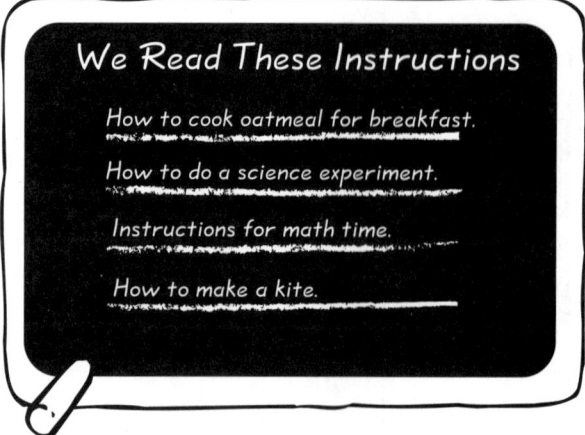

Listen to Instructions

Explain that many of the instructions they receive during the day require them to listen. Do one or more of the following activities to practice listening and follow instructions.

Do what I say:

Give simple oral instructions for the class to follow. Mix funny instructions with functional ones you commonly use. Begin with students seated at their desks or work tables.

"Stand up and push your chair under the table/desk."
"Stand on one foot and hop up and down."
"Stop hopping and tiptoe to the back of the classroom."
"Walk like a gorilla back to your chair."
"Pull out your chair and sit down quietly."

Follow these instructions:

Each student will need a sheet of blank paper, a pencil, and a box of crayons. Explain that you will give each instruction one time so they must listen carefully to everything you say.

Show students how to fold the paper into sixteen boxes. Have them number the boxes from 1 to 16, putting the numbers in the upper left-hand corner of each box. When the papers are ready, give instructions one at a time telling students what to do in each box. The complexity of the instructions will depend on the ability and age of your students. Here are some suggestions:

1. Write your first name in box 16.
2. Put a red X in box 5.
3. Draw a dog in the box before your name.
4. Make a yellow star in box 1.
5. Write the letter "z" in the box after the red X.
6. Put a black dot in box 11.
7. Draw a boat in box 3.
8. Write your last name in box 4.
9. Write your age old you are in box 2.
10. Put the number 99 in the box above the black dot.

Obstacle course:

Make a simple obstacle course in the classroom using masking tape, classroom furniture, and any other useful items you might have available. Select several students to line up at the beginning of the course. Give oral directions to guide them to the finish line.

"Walk along the line until you come to the table."
"Crawl under the table. Don't lift your head up!"
"Stand up and walk to the right of the line of chairs. Stop when you come to the box."
"Step in the box with both feet. Step out of the box and walk along the line to the left."
"Hop over the jump ropes and sit down on the rug."

Repeat with new directions and a new set of students.

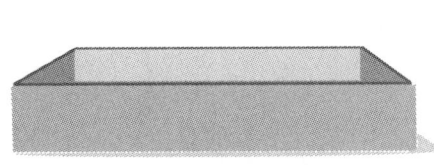

Read the Instructions

Now repeat one or more of the activities on the preceding page using word, phrase, and sentence cards showing the instructions.

Do what I say:
Make a set of cards containing instructions or reproduce those on pages 7–9.

Show the cards, one at a time, for the class (or an individual) to read and follow. Mix funny instructions with functional ones you commonly use.

Follow these instructions:
Reproduce the instructions on page 10. Students will also need a sheet of blank paper, a pencil, and crayons. Have them fold their paper into sixteen boxes and then read and follow their instruction sheet.

Home to the castle:
Reproduce page 11. This paper/pencil variation of an "obstacle course" requires students to read instructions to get the knight and princess from their ship, safely home to the castle.

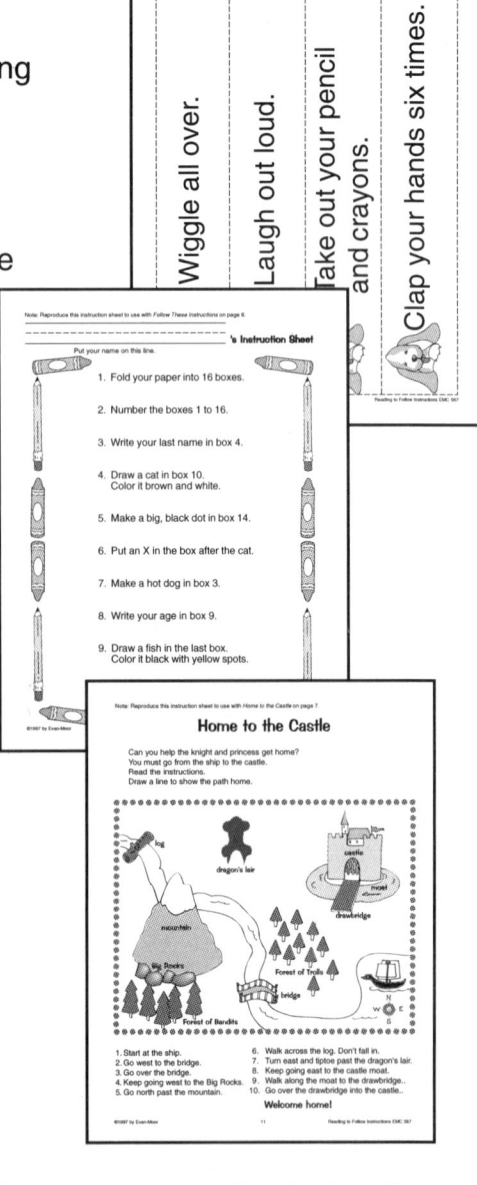

Which Was Easier?

When students have had a chance to experience both listening and reading instructions, ask "Which was easier/harder for you to do?" Explain that people take in information in different ways. No way is better; they are just different. Much of what we do at school requires us to listen to and read instructions. So it is important that we learn how to be both careful listeners and readers.

Introduce the "Following Instructions" chart on page 2. Discuss each step, explaining how and when to use it. Refer to the chart frequently when you are asking students to follow instructions.

Note: Reproduce these cards to use with *Do What I Say* on page 6. Paste the sentences on tag.

Stand up.

Sit down.

Line up at the door.

Hop on your left foot.

Note: Reproduce these cards to use with *Do What I Say* on page 6. Paste the sentences on tag.

- Wiggle all over.
- Laugh out loud.
- Take out your pencil and crayons.
- Clap your hands six times.

Passport to the Living Sea

Name:

Address:

School:

Phone #:

Favorite ocean activity:

S.S. 98

Captain Swanson
Welcome Abroad Crew

Note: Reproduce these cards to use with *Do What I Say* on page 6. Paste the sentences on tag.

- Set your chair on top of your desk.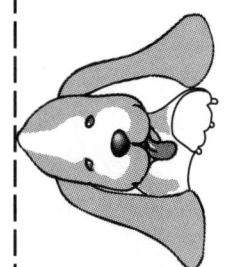
- Raise your hand if you can read this card.
- Turn and shake hands with your neighbor.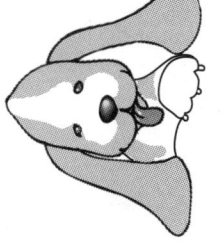
- Sit down and fold your hands in your lap.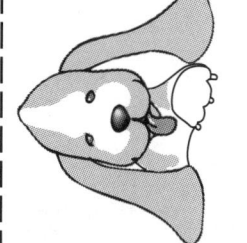

Note: Reproduce this instruction sheet to use with *Follow These Instructions* on page 6.

_____ 's Instruction Sheet

Put your name on this line.

1. Fold your paper into 16 boxes.

2. Number the boxes 1 to 16.

3. Write your last name in box 4.

4. Draw a cat in box 10.
   Color it brown and white.

5. Make a big, black dot in box 14.

6. Put an X in the box after the cat.

7. Make a hot dog in box 3.

8. Write your age in box 9.

9. Draw a fish in the last box.
   Color it black with yellow spots.

10. Make a Z in box 7.

Note: Reproduce this instruction sheet to use with *Home to the Castle* on page 6.

Home to the Castle

Can you help the knight and princess get home?
You must go from the ship to the castle.
Read the instructions.
Draw a line to show the path home.

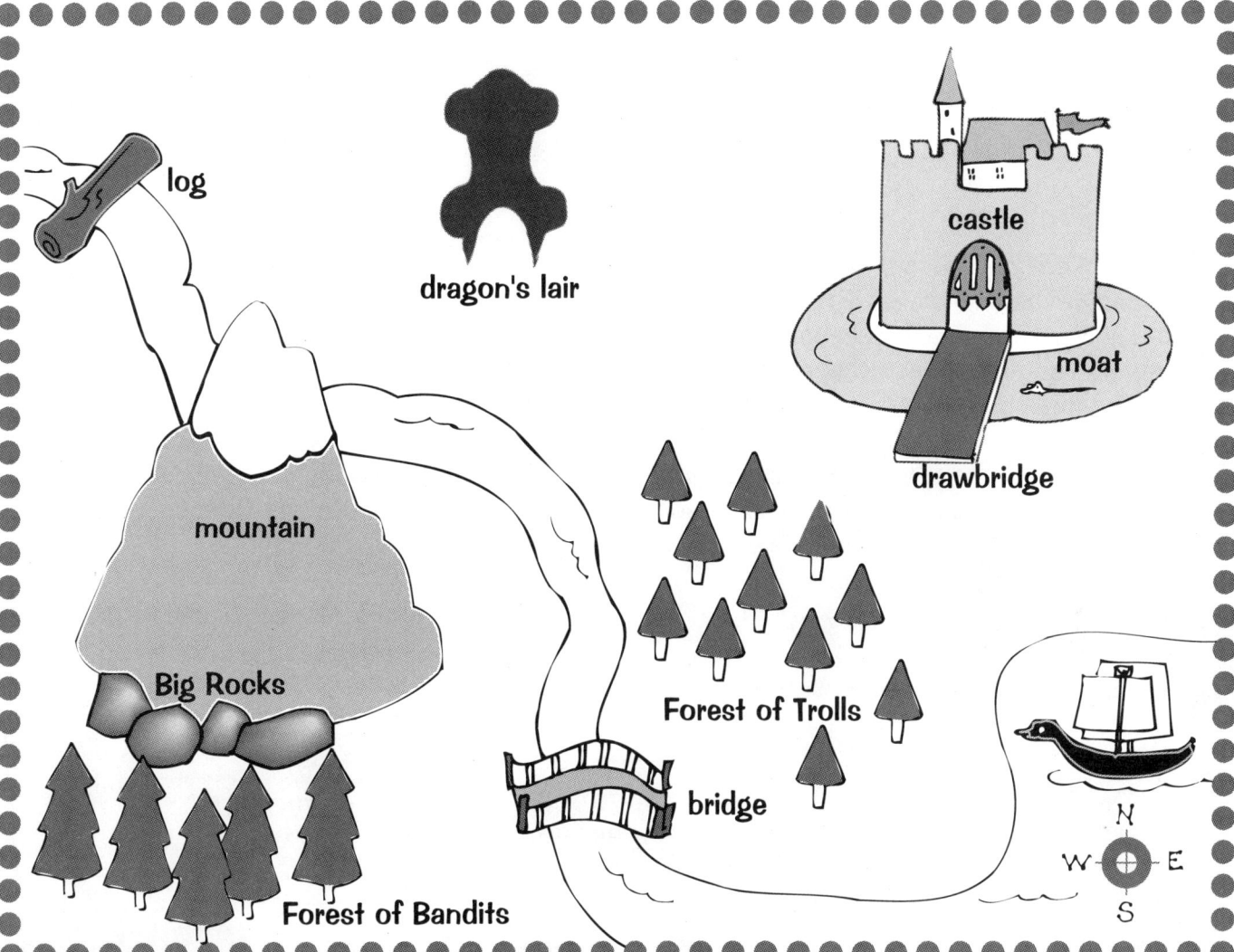

1. Start at the ship.
2. Go west to the bridge.
3. Go over the bridge.
4. Keep going west to the Big Rocks.
5. Go north past the mountain.
6. Walk across the log. Don't fall in.
7. Turn east and tiptoe past the dragon's lair.
8. Keep going east to the castle moat.
9. Walk along the moat to the drawbridge.
10. Go over the drawbridge into the castle.

Welcome home!

At School

A typical day in the classroom provides many opportunities to read instructions for real purposes.

Daily Directions

Write messages on the chalkboard throughout the day, giving general directions such as "Sit down and take out your reading log," "Get your library book and line up at the door," or "Put your work away and get ready for lunch."

In the beginning, read the messages together and discuss the instructions that were included. As students' reading skills become better, observe who successfully reads and follows the instructions on their own.

Daily Problems

Put up a daily problem or task in various subjects. These may be placed on charts or written on the chalkboard. Explain the process you wish students to follow as they read and solve these daily problems. (Do they write down the problem and answer? Can they help one another? Will you check the answer together?" "Can they use counters when solving math problems?)

Students read and follow the instructions when upon entering class after recess, lunch, etc. (The bibliography contains a list of some Evan-Moor books that provide these type of problems.)

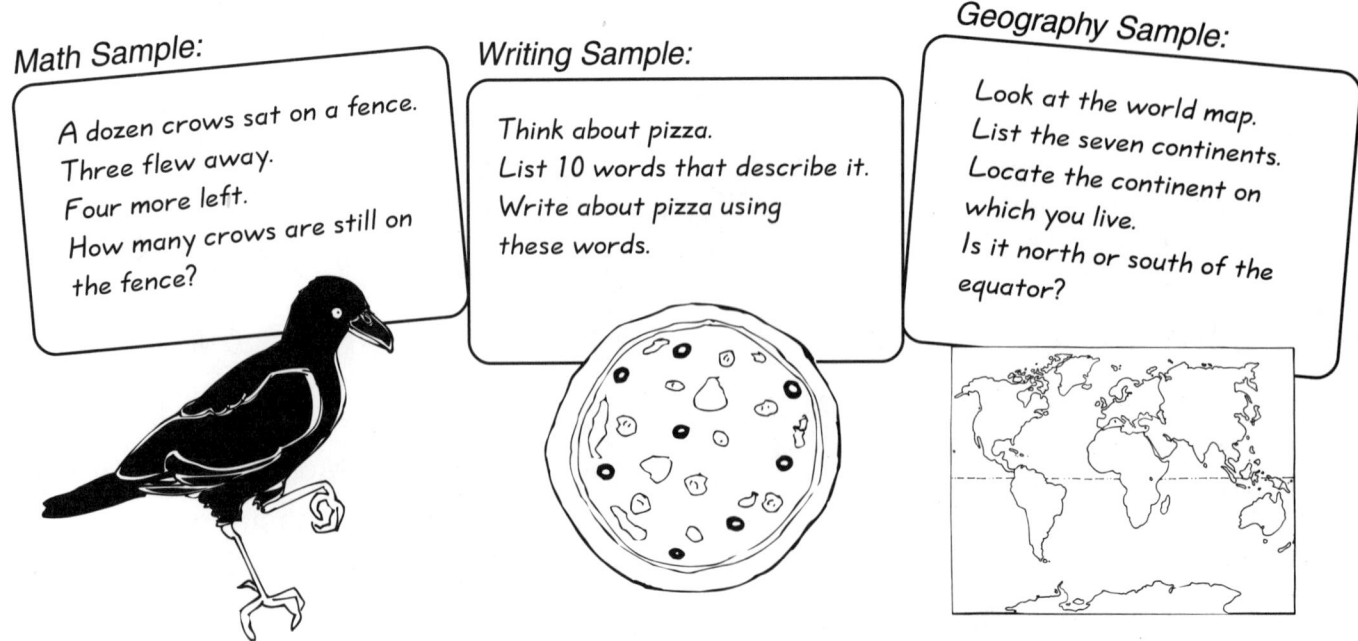

Math Sample:
A dozen crows sat on a fence.
Three flew away.
Four more left.
How many crows are still on the fence?

Writing Sample:
Think about pizza.
List 10 words that describe it.
Write about pizza using these words.

Geography Sample:
Look at the world map.
List the seven continents.
Locate the continent on which you live.
Is it north or south of the equator?

Developing Vocabulary

Students need to be able to read and understand words that give instructions. The words you choose to teach will depend on the ability of your students.

Make cards of the word and phrases you plan to introduce, or reproduce those on page 14. Use the cards in these ways:

1. Show each card. Read the term with your students. Discuss what each term means. Demonstrate each of the terms.

2. Put the cards into a sack. Select a student to pull out one card. The child gives clues, in actions or words, about the word chosen. The class tries to guess the word. Continue until all cards have been used.

3. Reproduce page 15 for additional practice.

Use these terms frequently in both oral and written instructions.

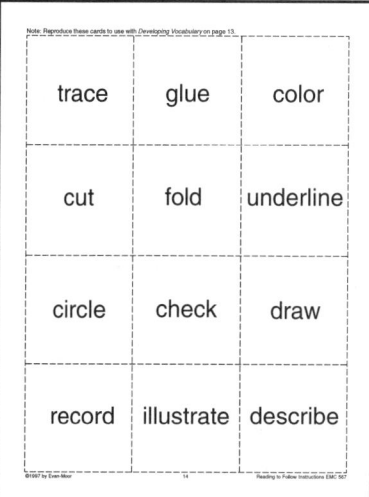

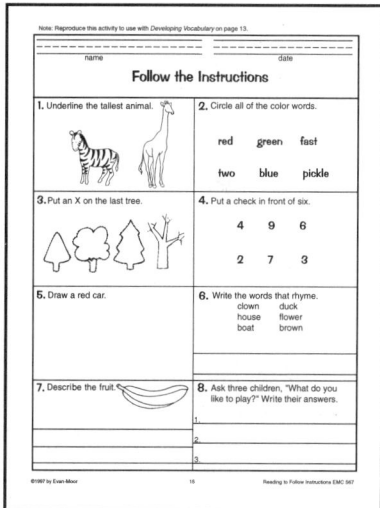

Reading Instructions on the Computer Screen

The computer is an excellent example of reading instructions in a real-life situation. Work together as a class to develop a list of computer terms and procedures used in your classroom. Select students to demonstrate these procedures to the rest of the class.

Observe students as they use the computer to see how well they follow the "instructions" provided by icons and words.

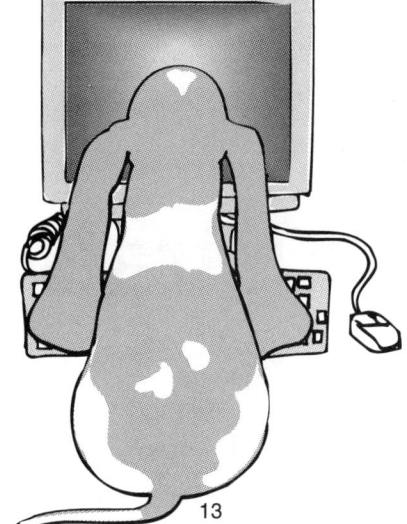

Note: Reproduce these cards to use with *Developing Vocabulary* on page 13.

trace	glue	color
cut	fold	underline
circle	check	draw
record	illustrate	describe

Note: Reproduce this activity to use with *Developing Vocabulary* on page 13.

name   date

Follow the Instructions

1. Underline the tallest animal.

2. Circle all of the color words.

red   green   fast

two   blue   pickle

3. Put an X on the last tree.

4. Put a check in front of six.

4   9   6

2   7   3

5. Draw a red car.

6. Write the words that rhyme.
clown   duck
house   flower
boat   brown

7. Describe the fruit.

8. Ask three children, "What do you like to play?" Write their answers.

1.

2.

3.

Writing Instructions

Reading and writing are both important components of literacy. As your students are learning to read instructions, require them to write instructions as well. This requires great attention to detail and sequence. Have your students practice these skills by doing one or more of the following activities. Start with short, simple steps. Increase the requirements for more able students.

How Did We Do It?

1. Have the students do a familiar task (draw a cat, put on a jacket, read a book, etc.). Then, as a class, have them tell you the steps they followed.

2. Write these on the chalkboard. When the instructions are complete, read them together to see what revisions must be made. Students often overlook the most obvious steps ("Take the lid off of the paste jar." "Get a piece of paper."). Continue reading and revising until everyone agrees the instructions are clear.

What Step Is Missing?

Reproduce page 18 for students to sequence directions for fixing a bowl of cereal and milk.

Explain that one step is missing. They must write this step themselves. Form partners to check their work.

©1997 by Evan-Moor 16 Reading to Follow Instructions EMC 567

How Do You Cook It?

Brainstorm to create a list of foods students have made for themselves. Use the term "cook" loosely for this activity. Fixing a slice of bread with peanut butter or making toast involves enough instructions for young recipe writers. Reproduce the recipe form on page 19.

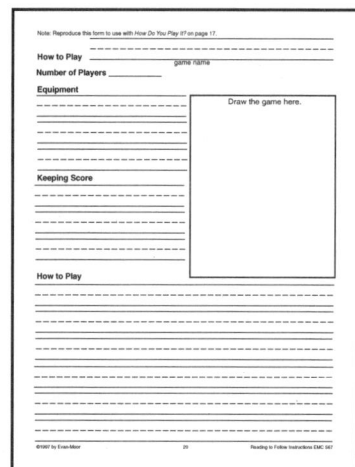

How Do You Play It?

Have students write the instructions for playing a favorite game. Before they begin, brainstorm to make a list of things to include (number of players, equipment, rules, keeping score). Reproduce the form on page 20 for this writing experience.

When they are finished, have students pair up to read and revise their directions.

Substitute Teacher Log

Have your students to write instructions for daily procedures. Explain that these must be clear and accurate so a substitute teacher would be able to follow them. Include:

- calendar
- fire drill procedures
- check out library books
- taking attendance
- taking lunch count

Have students work in groups, with each group responsible for one set of instructions. When all groups are finished, have them share what they have written to see if revisions are needed. When everyone is satisfied, place the instruction pages in your substitute folder.

©1997 by Evan-Moor — Reading to Follow Instructions EMC 567

Note: Reproduce this sequencing activity to use with page 16.

Fixing Cereal

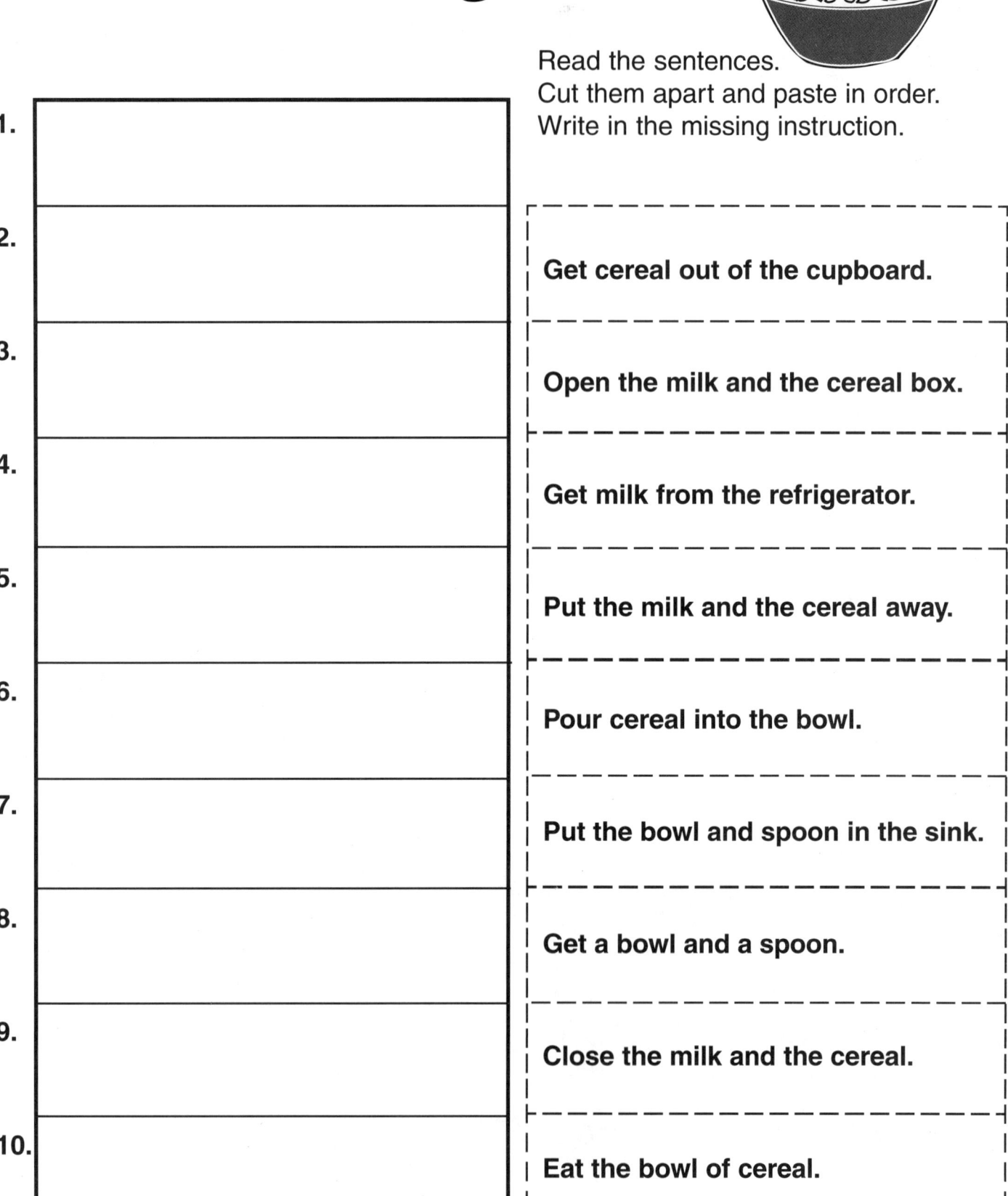

Read the sentences.
Cut them apart and paste in order.
Write in the missing instruction.

1.
2.
3.
4.
5.
6.
7.
8.
9.
10.

Get cereal out of the cupboard.

Open the milk and the cereal box.

Get milk from the refrigerator.

Put the milk and the cereal away.

Pour cereal into the bowl.

Put the bowl and spoon in the sink.

Get a bowl and a spoon.

Close the milk and the cereal.

Eat the bowl of cereal.

©1997 by Evan-Moor   18   Reading to Follow Instructions EMC 567

Note: Reproduce this form to use with *How Do You Cook It?* on page 17.

How to Make _____

recipe name

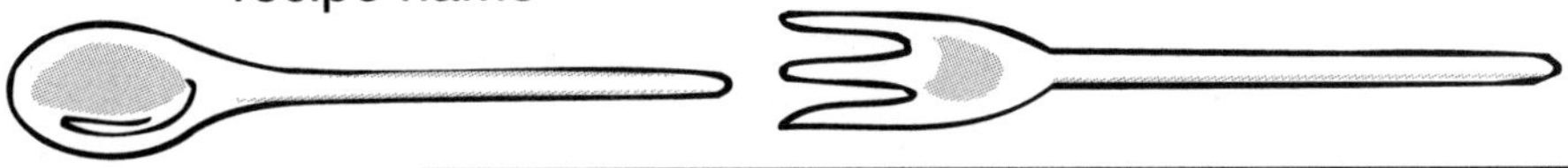

Get these ingredients:

_____

_____

_____

Draw the finished food here.

Get this equipment:

_____

_____

_____

Do this:

_____

_____

_____

_____

_____

_____

Note: Reproduce this form to use with *How Do You Play It?* on page 17.

How to Play _____
game name

Number of Players _____

Equipment

_____

Keeping Score

_____

| Draw the game here. |

How to Play

_____

©1997 by Evan-Moor — Reading to Follow Instructions EMC 567

Reading Instructions

In Math

Reading math equations or word problems is like reading instructions. They contain the clues to the procedures needed to solve the problems. Ask your students to analyze some problems.

What instructions are in this equation?
(The problem tells us to add the first two numbers and then to subtract the last number.)

$6 + 2 - 3 =$

What instructions are in this word problem?
(The problem tells us to find how many birds were left. Were left is a clue that tells us to subtract.)

8 birds were sitting on a fence.
My cat chased 3 of the birds away.
How many birds were left?

Explain that before beginning ANY math lesson, you need to read all of the instructions. If there is a word problem, read the problem carefully. If there are equations, read the signs carefully. Put these steps on a chart. Post it in class.

When you do math problems
1. *Read.*
2. *Think. What did it ask?*
3. *Do.*
4. *Read again.*
5. *Check your answer.*

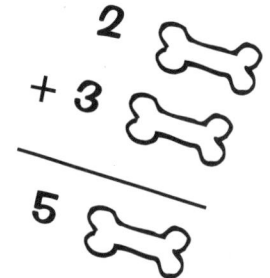

Class Practice

Do math problems together to practice reading instructions in math. Pages 22–24 contain sample problems at three levels of difficulty. Use any or all of these for practice with your students.

1. Make transparencies of the pages you wish to use or reproduce them for each student.

2. Read the directions with your class. Discuss what each step says to do.

3. Go back to the first step. Read it as a group. Have students do just that much. Continue this process with each of the remaining steps.

4. Read each step once more as students check to see that they followed that step.

Note: Make a transparency of these instructions to use for class practice with the activity on page 21.

Find the Answer

Problem:
2 + 8 - 5 =

1. Read the problem.

2. What do the signs tell you to do?

3. What do you have to do first?

4. What do you do next?

5. What is the answer?

Problem:
9 bones in a bowl.
A puppy ate 6 bones.
How many bones are left?

1. Read the problem.

2. What did it ask?

3. How many bones are in the bowl?
   Draw the bones.

4. How many bones did the puppy eat?
   Cross out (X) the bones the puppy ate.

5. How many bones are left?
   Count the bones with no X.

6. Read the problem again.
   Did you do all of the steps?

©1997 by Evan-Moor   Reading to Follow Instructions EMC 567

Note: Make a transparency of these instructions to use for class practice with the activity on page 21.

Bird Eggs

Problem:

Five birds each made a nest in the tree.
Two eggs are in each nest.
How many eggs are there in all?

1. Read the problem. What did it ask?

2. How many birds made nests?
   Draw the nests.

3. How many eggs are in each nest?
   Draw the eggs.

4. Count the eggs.
   How many eggs are there in all?

5. Read the problem again.
   Did you do all of the steps?

Bonus:
Can you think of two more ways to find the answer?

Note: Make a transparency of these instructions to use for class practice with the activity on page 21.

Letters in Our Names

Problem:

With which letter of the alphabet do the most names in class begin?

1. Write the letters of the alphabet in a row on the chalkboard.

2. Make a tally mark under the letter that each student's name starts with.

3. Count the tally marks for each letter.
   Write the numeral under the tally marks.

4. What is the answer to the problem?

5. Now answer these questions.
   How many names started with A?
   Did any names start with Z?
   How many names started with the same letter as your name?

©1997 by Evan-Moor — Reading to Follow Instructions EMC 567

In Science

The general instructions for all science experiments should include:

- a materials list
- safety rules
- a hypothesis or question
- a way to record observations
- experiment directions
- cleanup requirements

Class Practice

Model the procedure for reading instructions in science by doing the experiment on page 26 with your students.

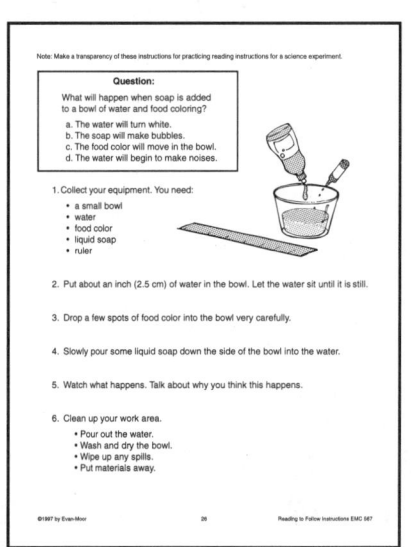

1. Make a transparency of the instructions on page 26 or reproduce the page for each group of students. Prepare a set of materials for each group conducting the experiment.

2. Divide the class into groups of four. Give each child in the group a number. Explain that child #1 will do the first step (collect needed materials). Child #2 will do step two and so on. Everyone will help with cleanup.

3. Read the question to be answered by the experiment. Discuss what is being asked. Read the four possible answers. Have each group decide what they think will happen.

4. Read through the instructions with your students. Discuss what is to be done at each step.

5. Go back to the first instruction. Read it with your students and have child #1 in each group do the step.

6. Go on to the next instruction. Call on child #2 to do that step. Continue until all instructions have been completed. Record each group's results.

7. Go back through all of the steps to check that they were done. Discuss what might happen if you misread a direction or skipped one.

Note: Make a transparency of these instructions for practicing reading instructions for a science experiment.

Question:

What will happen when soap is added to a bowl of water and food coloring?

a. The water will turn white.
b. The soap will make bubbles.
c. The food color will move in the bowl.
d. The water will begin to make noises.

1. Collect your equipment. You need:
   - a small bowl
   - water
   - food color
   - liquid soap
   - ruler

2. Put about an inch (2.5 cm) of water in the bowl. Let the water sit until it is still.

3. Drop a few spots of food color into the bowl very carefully.

4. Slowly pour some liquid soap down the side of the bowl into the water.

5. Watch what happens. Talk about why you think this happens.

6. Clean up your work area.
   - Pour out the water.
   - Wash and dry the bowl.
   - Wipe up any spills.
   - Put materials away.

Reading Instructions: For Cooking

Instructions in cooking can be something as simple as opening a package (open this end, etc.) to preparing an elaborate recipe.

Cooking Terms

Cooking has a vocabulary of its own. There are special names for equipment, procedures, and measurement. Introduce these terms before beginning cooking experiences.

1. Brainstorm to make a list of terms students already know. Record these under these headings on chart paper. Add new terms as they are learned.

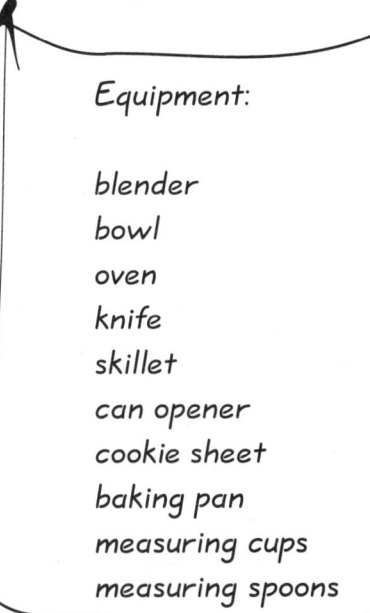

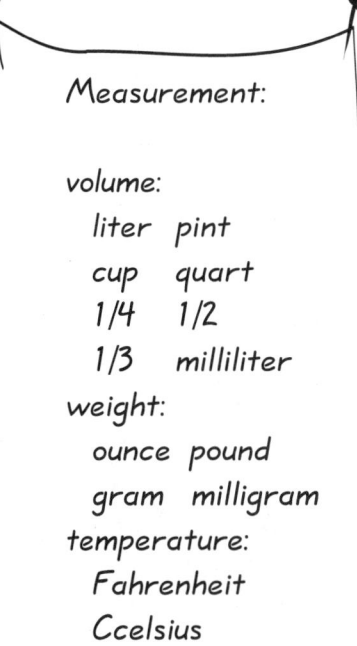

Equipment:
- blender
- bowl
- oven
- knife
- skillet
- can opener
- cookie sheet
- baking pan
- measuring cups
- measuring spoons

Procedures:
- mix
- pour
- bend
- stir
- slice
- chop
- bake
- boil
- cool
- freeze

Measurement:
- volume:
  - liter pint
  - cup quart
  - 1/4 1/2
  - 1/3 milliliter
- weight:
  - ounce pound
  - gram milligram
- temperature:
  - Fahrenheit
  - Ccelsius

2. Set up a display of real items or pictures labeled with their names. Point to each item and have students give its name and describe its use.

3. Have students help make a matching game using the cooking terms. Assign one cooking term to each child. Give each child a 4" X 6 " (10 X 15 cm) card. Fold the card in half. Draw a picture to illustrate the word on one half of the card and write the term on the other half. Cut all the cards in half and place them in a box. Place the box in a center for independent matching practice.

Reading Instructions on Packages

Bring in an assortment of packages containing preparation instructions. Instant pudding, microwave popcorn, instant soup, muffins, etc., all have fairly simple instructions to follow. (Ask parents to send in empty boxes or buy samples.)

Divide the class into groups. Have each group read the instructions on one or two packages. Each group will then present their item to the class and explain how it is to be prepared.

Place the containers on a table for students to use as part of "reading the room."

Before You Cook

Make a chart of general instructions (page 30) to be followed any time students cook in class.

Let's Cook

Provide experiences in food preparation (and eating) in class. Have students work in small groups when they cook.

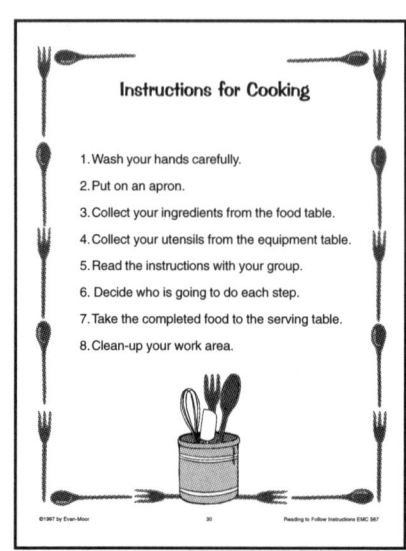

1. Teach students how to use the necessary equipment (use only plastic knives) and how to mix and measure ingredients.

2. Provide ingredients, equipment, and a recipe (instructions) for each group. Invite parents to act as "cooking assistants."

3. Have each group prepare the same recipe for their own group or have each group prepare a different recipe, making enough for the whole class.

4. Discuss how to divide the tasks among the members of the group. One way would be to assign one person for each of these tasks — collect materials, read the recipe, mix the ingredients, divide into servings.

Making packaged foods:
These work well for small groups and many can be put in a center for independent cooking experiences. Students might make muffins from a mix, for example.

You will need to provide:
- toaster oven
- wooden spoon
- eggs
- package of muffin mix
- mixing bowl
- muffin tins
- water

Have the group read the chart of general instructions (page 30), and then read and follow the preparation steps on the package. An adult needs to be responsible for putting the muffins in the oven and removing them.

Reading recipes:
Make a collection of simple recipes to use for classroom cooking practice. (There are many recipe books available for children.)

Collect recipes that relate to a unit of study or piece of literature you plan to share with your students (churn butter, johnny cakes, Hoppin' John, etc.).

Two simple recipes are provided on page 31. Use these for two separate "cooking" experience or have half of the class do each recipe. After everyone has had a chance to cook and eat, pass out copies of page 32. Have students write out the steps they followed to prepare the food.

Instructions for Cooking

1. Wash your hands carefully.
2. Put on an apron.
3. Collect your ingredients from the food table.
4. Collect your utensils from the equipment table.
5. Read the instructions with your group.
6. Decide who is going to do each step.
7. Take the completed food to the serving table.
8. Clean up your work area.

Note: Use these recipes with the activity on page 29.

Triangle Sandwiches
(serves one)

Ingredients:
- slice of bread
- peanut butter
- jam

Equipment:
- paper plate
- 1 plastic knife
- plastic spoons

Do this:
1. Take a slice of bread.
2. Open the peanut butter and jam jars.
3. Put one spoonful of peanut butter on the bread. Spread it with your knife.
4. Put one spoonful of jam on the bread. Spread it with your knife.
5. Cut the sandwich into triangles.
6. Put the lid on the peanut butter and jam.
7. Clean up your work space.
8. Eat your sandwich. Yum!

Ants on a Log
(serves one)

Ingredients:
- 10 raisins
- creamy peanut butter
- celery
- 3" (7.5 cm) piece of celery

Equipment:
- plastic knife
- plastic spoon
- paper plate

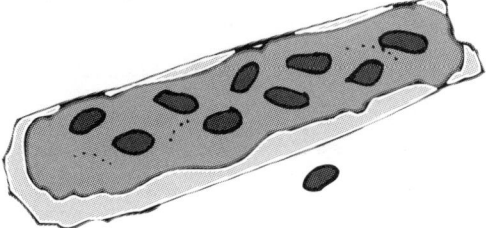

Do this:
1. Open the peanut butter jar.
2. Take a stalk of celery.
3. Put one spoonful of peanut butter on the celery. Spread it with your knife.
4. Open the raisin box. Take 10 raisins. Put them on the peanut butter.
5. Close the raisin box.
6. Put the lid on the peanut butter jar.
7. Clean up your work space.
8. Eat your "ants on a log."

Note: Reproduce this form to use with the activity on page 29.

Making _____
           food name   **Yum!**

This is what I used:

This is how I made it:

This is what
it looked like.

Note: "Gomoku" is from *Japan* by Betsy Franco (Evan-Moor, 1993)

 **Reading Instructions**

For Playing a Game

Provide a variety of board and card games for your students to use. Point out where the instructions for the games are written. (If they are too complicated for your students, write a simpler version and tape to the box).

At the Game Center

- Make a chart listing rules for game time. Post the chart near where the games are kept.
- List when games can be played.
- List how long the same group of children can play the game.
- Set "noise" parameters for game time.
- Develop steps for settling differences arising during play.

Game Time Rules

You may play a game when all your work is done.

You may play a game only once if others are waiting.

Quiet voices only, please.

Spin, roll, or flip to see who goes first.

Ask another student if you need help to settle a disagreement.

Reading Instructions to Play Gomoku (a Game from Japan)

1. Make a transparency of the playing board on the next page.

2. Reproduce one copy of the board for every two students.

3. Write the Gomoku rules on a chart or the chalkboard.

4. Place the transparency on your overhead projector. Explain the "Go" means five and "moku" means intersection. Show students the "intersections" on the board. Demonstrate drawing a circle at an intersection.

5. Read the game rules with the class, discussing what each step means.

6. Call a child to play one game with you as the class reads the instructions again.

7. When the demonstration game is over, read the game rules one more time, and have students play a game with the partner.

Gomoku Rules

1. Get a partner.
2. You need a playing board and two crayons.
   Each player uses a different color.
3. Take turns drawing circles on the board. You must draw at an intersection.
4. The winner is the first player to have five in a row. You can make your circles these ways.

across   down   corner to corner

5. Try to keep the other player from putting five in a row.

Note: Reproduce this grid to use as a playing board for Gomoku.

Gomoku
Five in a Row

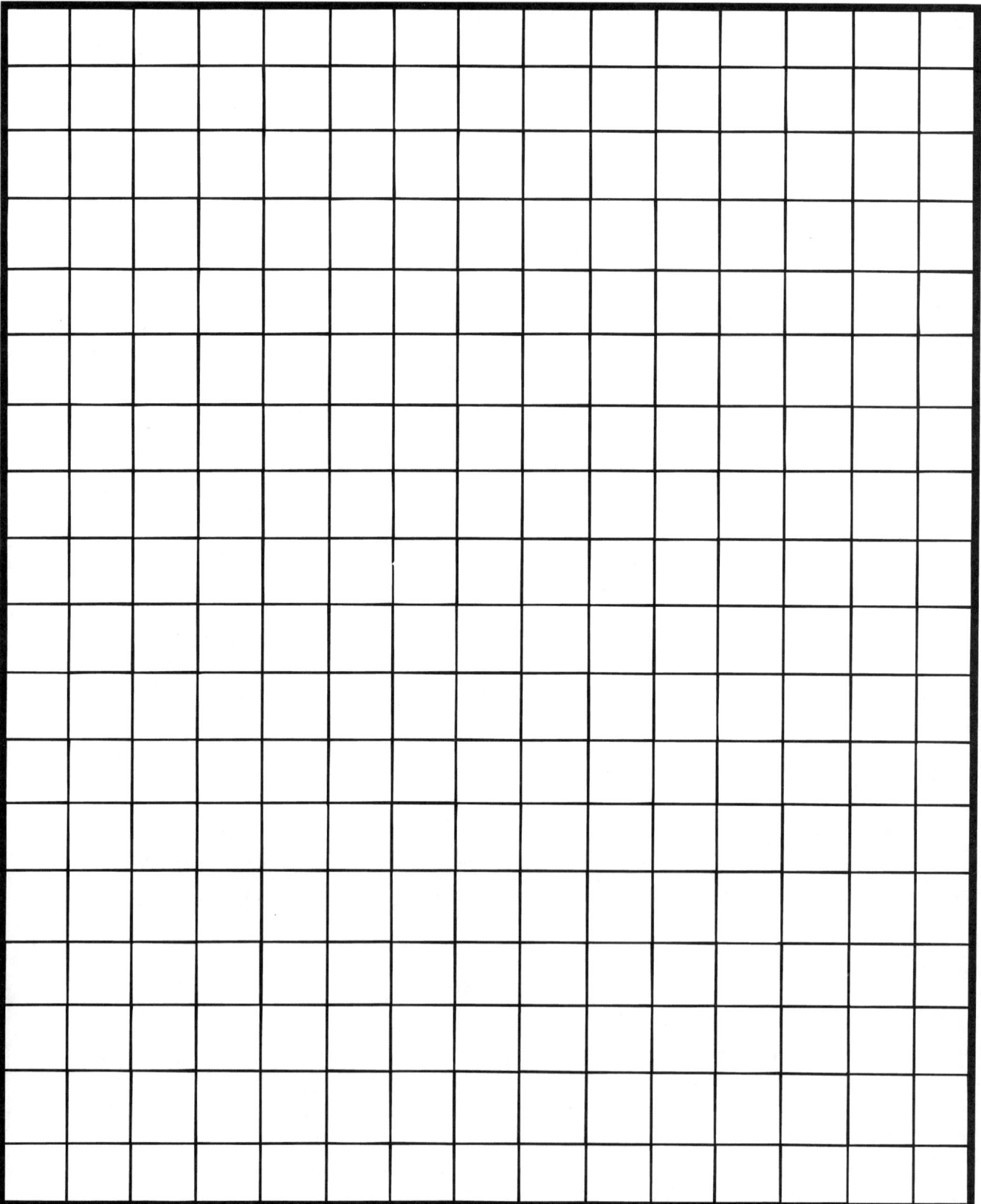

©1997 by Evan-Moor — Reading to Follow Instructions EMC 567

Reading Instructions: To Get from Here to There

Using Positional Words in Instructions

Students need to learn to read words that give instructions for finding one's way around. Words such as these are used on signs, in literature, and on activity sheets.

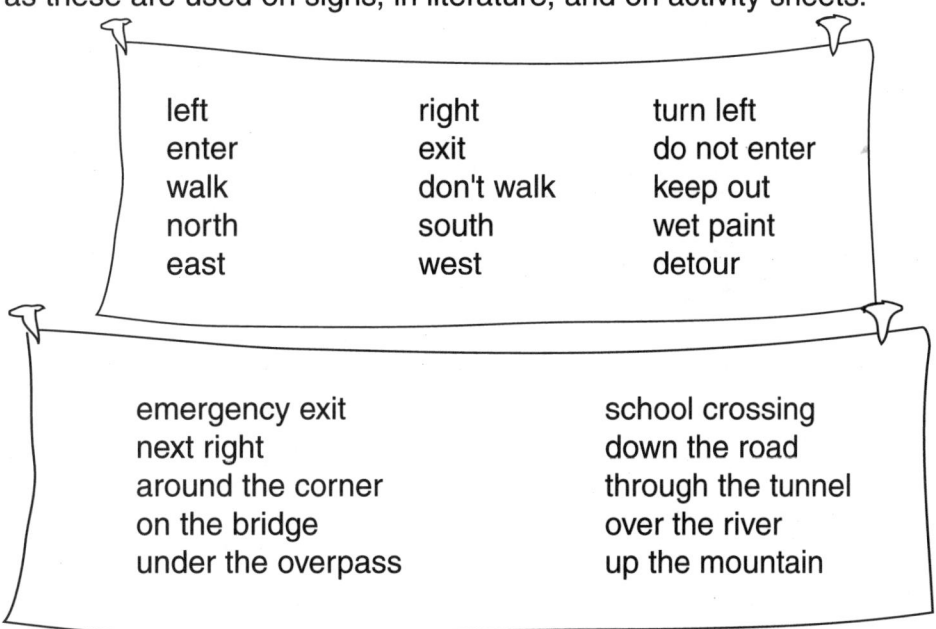

left	right	turn left
enter	exit	do not enter
walk	don't walk	keep out
north	south	wet paint
east	west	detour

emergency exit	school crossing
next right	down the road
around the corner	through the tunnel
on the bridge	over the river
under the overpass	up the mountain

Write the words and phrases on sentence strips. Use them in the ways suggested below.

1. Show each card. Read it with your students. Discuss what the word or phrase means. Have students read aloud as you go through the cards again.

2. Display several of the cards. Give information about one of the words at a time. Select a student to give the word you are describing.

   "This word says you can go through the door." (enter)
   "This word tells you not to go yet." (stop)
   "This phrase tells to be careful because children might be in the road."(school crossing)

©1997 by Evan-Moor

Reading Instructions to Find Places on Maps and Globes

1. Introduce the compass to your students. Have them work together in small groups using a compass to locate the four directions in your classroom. Post signs marking north, south, east, and west.

   Have everyone stand. Show a card with a direction written on it. Have students all turn in that direction. Then show a card to one child and ask him/her to go stand on that side of the classroom. Vary the activity by asking students to read two or more word cards and go to those sides of the room in order.

2. Make a simple map of the classroom. Laminate it. Post the map at a level students can reach. Put out a supply of erasable marking pens. Make a set of instructions on sentence strips. (Use a difficulty level appropriate for your students.) To introduce the map activity, show a strip, have any child read it and locate that place on the map. For example:

   "Put an X on the sink."
   "Draw a line from the computer to your desk."
   "Start at the door. Draw a line to the pencil sharpener."
   "Make a line over the desks on the south side of the room."

   Leave the map, pens, and sentence strips out for students to use for independent practice.

3. Provide a globe and a world map. Write instructions for locating places on sentence strips. Read one strip at a time with your students. Select someone to follow the instruction using the globe or map.

   "Is all of the water on the globe the same color?"
   "Do you live north or south of the equator?"
   "Find the country you live in on the map."
   "What color is the continent of Africa on the map?"
   "Is the North Pole at the top or bottom of the globe?"
   "Name the seven continents."
   "Which direction would you go to get from Canada to Brazil?"

   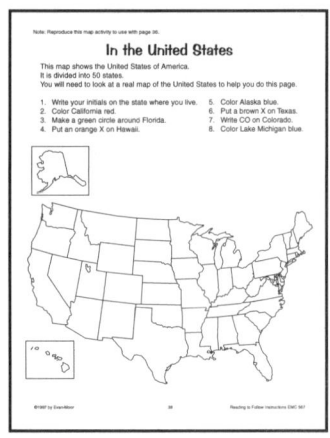

4. Reproduce the maze on page 37 and the map on page 38 for additional practice in reading instructions to find places.

Note: Reproduce this maze activity to use with page 36.

Escape from the Maze

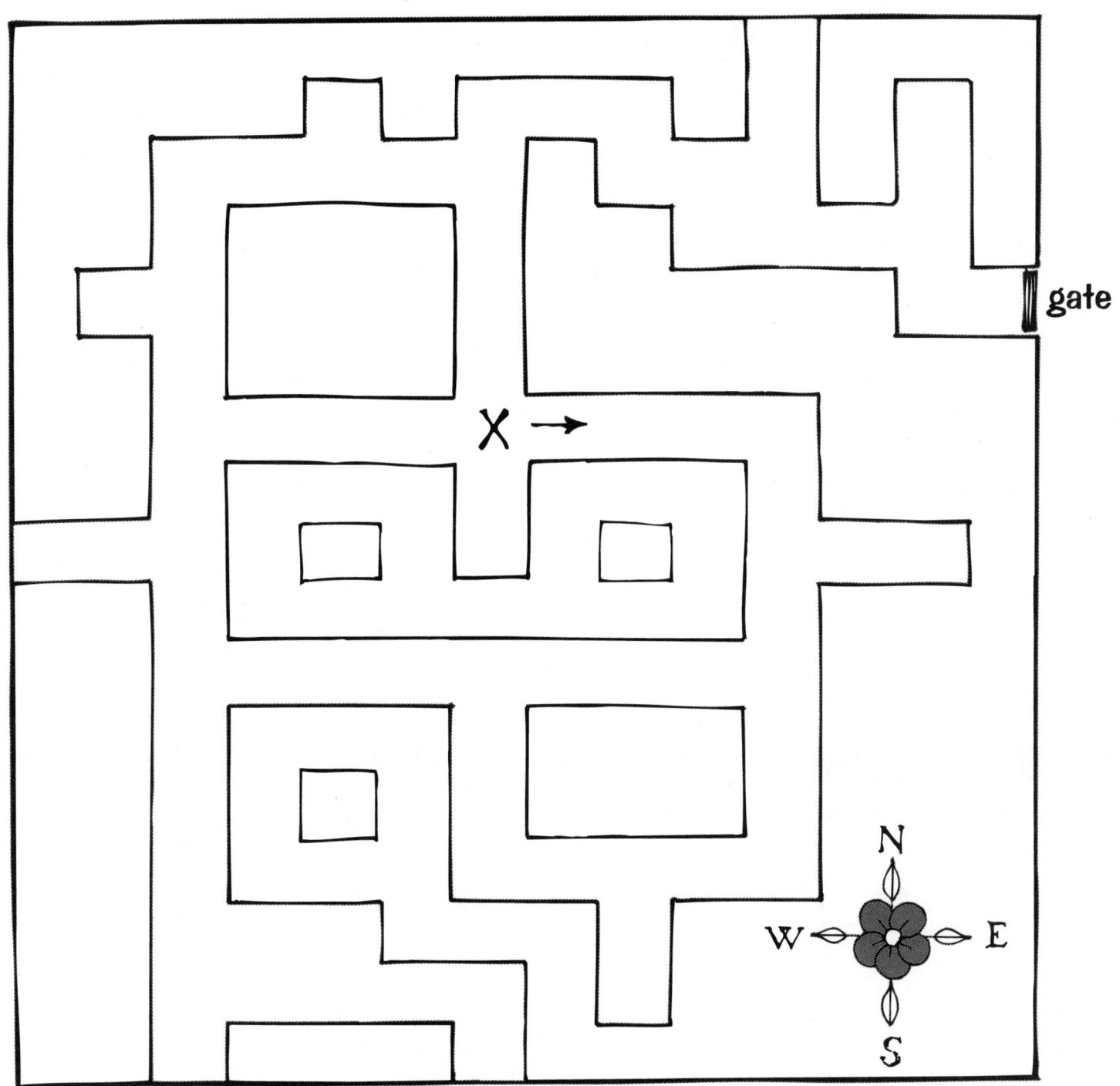

Follow these instructions to get out of the maze.
1. Start at the X.
2. Go east to the wall.
3. Now go south as far as you can.
4. Turn west.
5. Go north.
6. Now go west again.
7. Go north as far as you can, and then turn east.
8. Can you find your way to the gate now?

©1997 by Evan-Moor 37 Reading to Follow Instructions EMC 567

Note: Reproduce this map activity to use with page 36.

In the United States

This map shows the United States of America.
It is divided into 50 states.
You will need to look at a real map of the United States to help you do this page.

1. Write your initials on the state where you live.
2. Color California red.
3. Make a green circle around Florida.
4. Put an orange X on Hawaii.
5. Color Alaska blue.
6. Put a brown X on Texas.
7. Write CO on Colorado.
8. Color Lake Michigan blue.

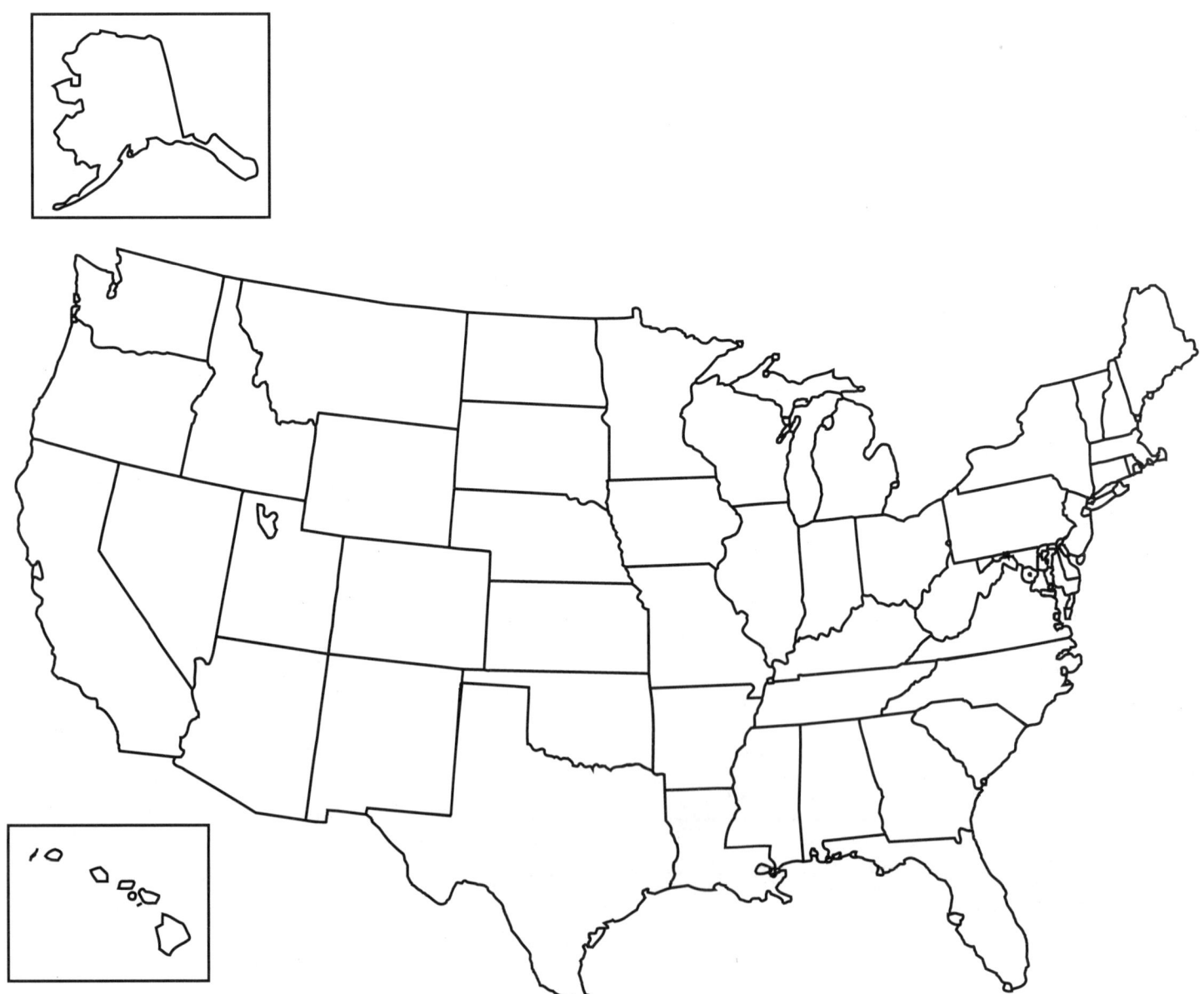

Put It Together

Some Assembly Required

Show pictures or samples of things that have to be put together — model airplane or car, doll house, pattern pieces for making a clothing item, prefabricated bookcase, bicycle, toy, etc. Explain what parts had to be put together in these samples.

Discuss the types of things students and/or their parents have had to put together. Ask how they knew what to do (read instructions). Invite students to bring in something they have put together to share with the class.

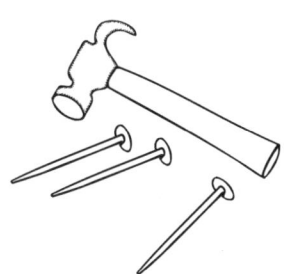

Let's Put It Together

Bring in a new model, materials for a book shelf, or other item requiring some assembly. Read the instructions with your class. Have them help assemble the object.

Reproduce page 40 for additional practice in reading instructions to put something together.

Assembly Center

Provide building toys such as an Erector® set or Lego® blocks that come with building instructions (or make your own sets of instructions on task cards). Place these in an area with where students can explore reading instructions to build things.

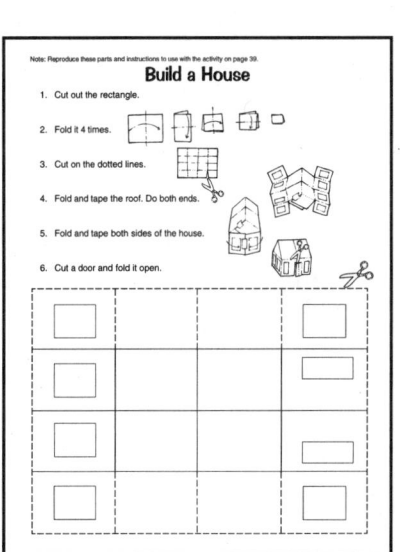

©1997 by Evan-Moor

Note: Reproduce these parts and instructions to use with the activity on page 39.

Build a House

1. Cut out the rectangle.

2. Fold it 4 times.

3. Cut on the dotted lines.

4. Fold and tape the roof. Do both ends.

5. Fold and tape both sides of the house.

6. Cut a door and fold it open.

In Art

Add a new element to your art activities by giving students written instructions to read and follow. These instructions can be a combination of pictures and words.

Make a Stamp

Model reading instructions by making stamps for printing. Each student will need:

- scissors
- glue
- pencil
- large wooden bead
- a stamp pad (can be shared)
- scratch paper - 3" square (7.5 cm)
- foam shoe inner sole - 3" square (7.5 cm)
- cardboard - 4" square (10 cm)
- construction paper - 6" X 9" (15 X 23 cm)

1. Make a transparency of page 42 or reproduce the page for each student.

2. Read all of the instructions together as a group. Discuss the meaning of terms such as: design, inner sole, handle.

3. Go through the steps one at a time as students create a simple design and make a stamp.

4. Use the completed stamp to make patterns on construction paper. (The stamps can also be used to make designs on tee shirts (using fabric paint), stationary, or greeting cards.)

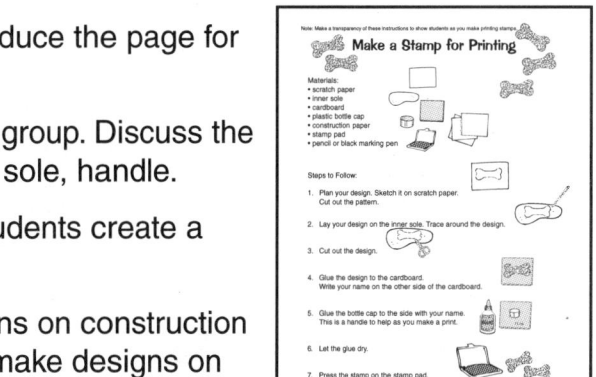

Read and Draw

Make a set of task cards containing instructions for drawing. (Six sample cards can be found on page 43.)

Write one set of instructions on the chalkboard for everyone to follow as practice.

Place the cards in a drawing center. Include a supply of blank cards where students can write a set of directions for classmates to follow.

Drawing Challenges

Drawing challenges give instructions for "thinking about" the topic before following the drawing "challenge." Page 44 contains three examples to reproduce for your young artists.

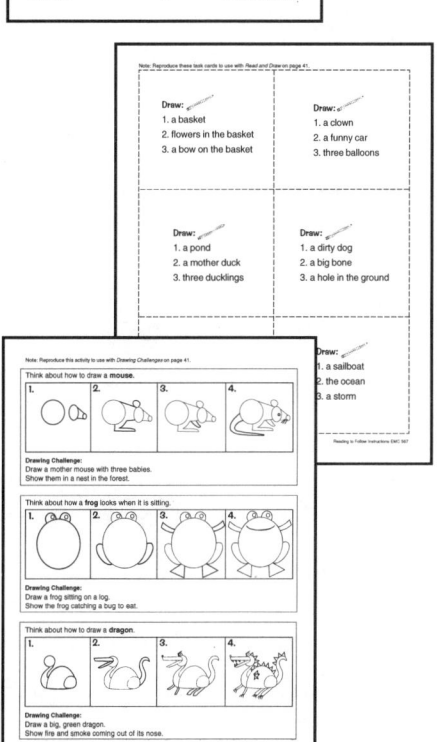

©1997 by Evan-Moor

Note: Make a transparency of these instructions to show students as you make printing stamps.

Make a Stamp for Printing

Materials:
- scratch paper
- inner sole
- cardboard
- plastic bottle cap
- construction paper
- stamp pad
- pencil or black marking pen

Steps to Follow:

1. Plan your design. Sketch it on scratch paper. Cut out the pattern.

2. Lay your design on the inner sole. Trace around the design.

3. Cut out the design.

4. Glue the design to the cardboard. Write your name on the other side of the cardboard.

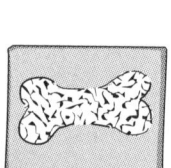

5. Glue the bottle cap to the side with your name. This is a handle to help as you make a print.

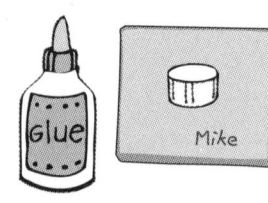

6. Let the glue dry.

7. Press the stamp on the stamp pad. Make a pattern on the construction paper.

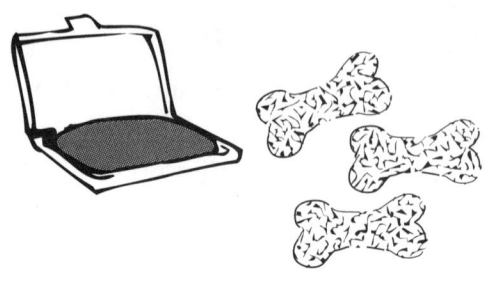

©1997 by Evan-Moor
Reading to Follow Instructions EMC 567

Note: Reproduce these task cards to use with *Read and Draw* on page 41.

Draw:
1. a basket
2. flowers in the basket
3. a bow on the basket

Draw:
1. a clown
2. a funny car
3. three balloons

Draw:
1. a pond
2. a mother duck
3. three ducklings

Draw:
1. a dirty dog
2. a big bone
3. a hole in the ground

Draw:
1. the sky
2. white clouds
3. a flying machine

Draw:
1. a sailboat
2. the ocean
3. a storm

Note: Reproduce this activity to use with *Drawing Challenges* on page 41.

Think about how to draw a **mouse.**

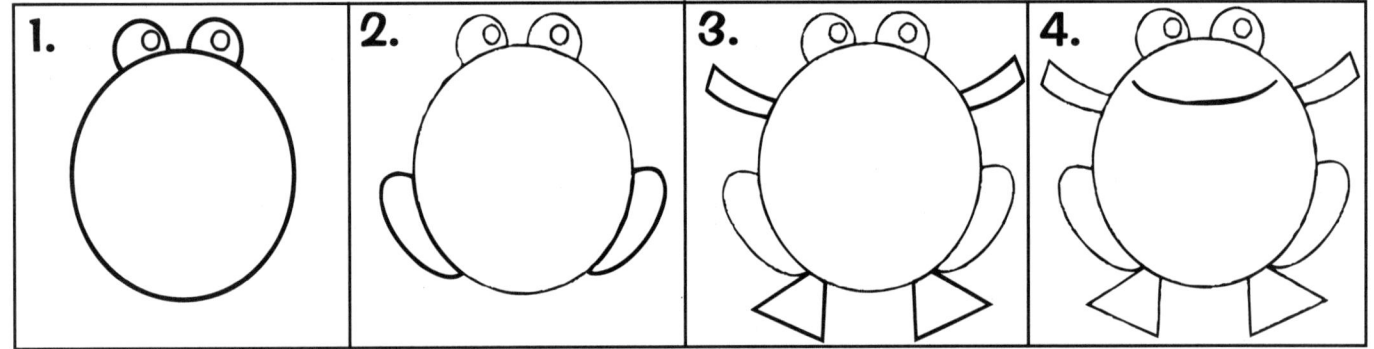

Drawing Challenge:
Draw a mother mouse with three babies.
Show them in a nest in the forest.

Think about how a **frog** looks when it is sitting.

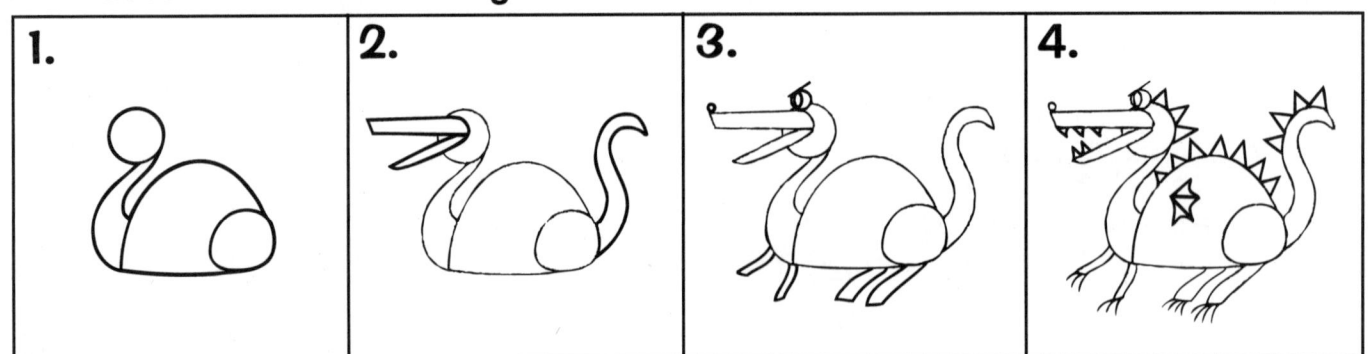

Drawing Challenge:
Draw a frog sitting on a log.
Show the frog catching a bug to eat.

Think about how to draw a **dragon.**

Drawing Challenge:
Draw a big, green dragon.
Show fire and smoke coming out of its nose.

Reading Instructions

At Home

Brainstorm all of the places and ways one might find and use instructions at home. Record these on a chart. Some will be as simple as "On-Off" instructions on appliances. Other may be as complicated as assembly instructions for a new bike.

We follow instructions:
- *on the refrigerator door*
- *on the answering machine*
- *on games*
- *in recipes*
- *to do homework*

Finding Instructions at Home

Have students look at home for places with instructions. (They don't need to read the instructions, just identify where they are.) Have them share the places they found. Record any new places on the chart started in the previous activity.

Interview

Reproduce the form on page 46. Have students interview eight people, asking the question, "What instructions did you have to read today?" Have students record the answers on their forms. When the record forms are returned to school, make a tally chart showing the answers. Compare how often various types of instructions were followed.

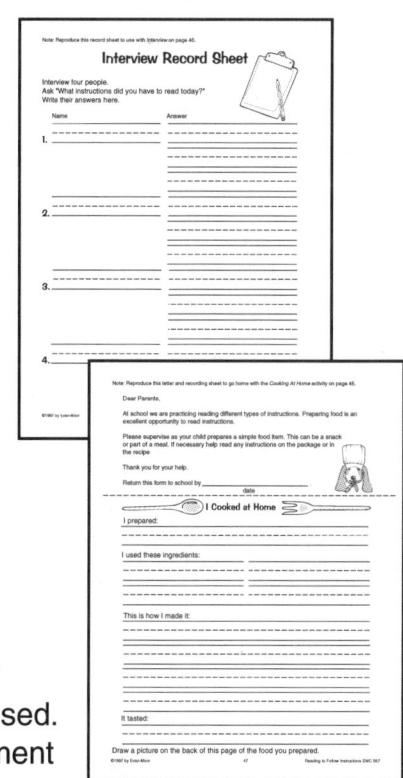

```
prepare a recipe      ₦₦ )
play a game           ) ) )
fix a leaking faucet  )
sew a dress           )
find directions using a map  ) )
store a can of paint  ) ) )
```

Cooking at Home

1. Discuss the types of cooking experiences your students have had at home. Some will have done little more than pour cold cereal into a bowl. Others may already be budding "chefs" with quite a bit of experience.

2. Send a copy of the letter and form on page 47 home, asking parents to supervise as the child reads instructions and cooks something. Have students return the form, along with a copy of recipe or the cooking instructions from the food package they used. Provide time for students to discuss the ingredients and equipment they used and to describe the steps they followed.

Note: Reproduce this record sheet to use with *Interview* on page 45.

Interview Record Sheet

Interview four people.
Ask "What instructions did you have to read today?"
Write their answers here.

Name Answer

1.

2.

3.

4.

Note: Reproduce this letter and recording sheet to go home with the *Cooking At Home* activity on page 45.

Dear Parents,

At school we are practicing reading different types of instructions. Preparing food is an excellent opportunity to read instructions.

Please supervise as your child prepares a simple food item. This can be a snack or part of a meal. If necessary help your child read any instructions on the package or in the recipe.

Thank you for your help.

Return this form to school by _____ .
                                      date

I Cooked at Home

I prepared: _____
_____
_____

I used these ingredients: _____ _____
_____ _____
_____ _____
_____ _____

This is how I made it: _____
_____
_____
_____
_____
_____
_____

It tasted: _____
_____
_____

Draw a picture on the back of this page of the food you prepared.

©1997 by Evan-Moor   Reading to Follow Instructions EMC 567

Reading Instructions

At Learning Centers

Centers provide a perfect place for independent practice in reading instructions.

Pages 50 - 64 contain six center activities for various areas of the curriculum. Each one contains teacher instructions, student instruction sheet, and other reproducible materials where needed. The teacher instruction sheet lists prior knowledge students will need to do the activity.

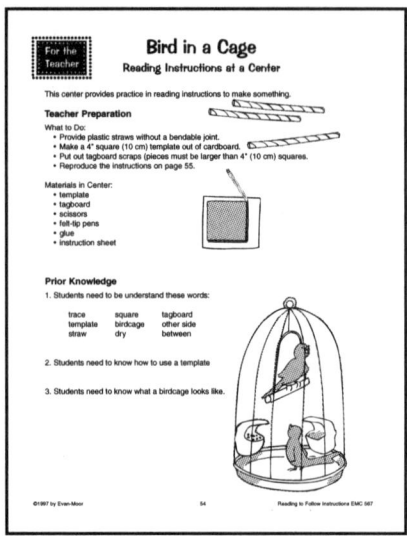

Prepare Centers

1. Make a sign of basic center instructions:

    • number of people who can be at the center at one time
    • how long an individual can stay at the center
    • general procedures — where to put completed projects, cleanup procedures, etc.

2. Provide materials and instruction sheets for the specific center activity.

Center Instructions

Number of people - 2

How long? - 20 minutes

1. Read instructions
2. Finish task
3. Put it in your cubby
4. Put everything away

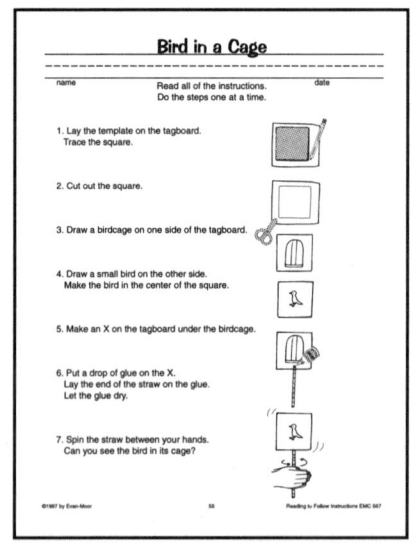

Center Standards

Develop with your class a set of center standards for working in the centers. List these standards on a chart and post it near your center work area. You need to:

• determine whether there will be a time limit for center work
• decide how participants will be chosen
• demonstrate appropriate use of the equipment in a center
• outline cleanup procedures
• discuss acceptable behavior when working at a center

©1997 by Evan-Moor   Reading to Follow Instructions EMC 567

Introduce Centers

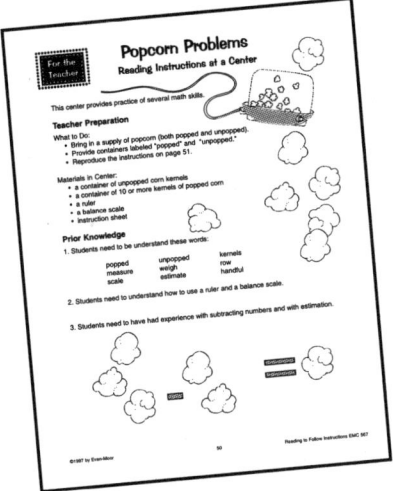 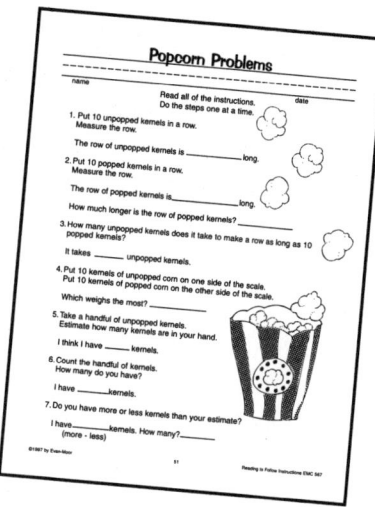

Present each center to students. Point out the materials in the center. Review the instruction sheet. Discuss center standards.

Prior Knowledge

1. Each center requires students to use skills and/or equipment. Review the skills required in the center as you introduce it. Select students to demonstrate equipment use.

2. The teacher instruction sheet for each center contains some words that may not be in your students' reading vocabulary. These words will need to be introduced before students do the center task.

   Write the words on a chart. Read each word and discuss its meaning. (Use actual items to show the meaning whenever possible.) Post the chart by the center. Encourage students to help one another read difficult words.

Observe Students During Center Work

Observe students carefully and assess their ability to read and follow the instructions given. Use the skills checklist on page 3 to record your observations at center time.

Popcorn Problems
Reading Instructions at a Center

This center provides practice of several math skills.

Teacher Preparation

What to do:
- Bring in a supply of popcorn (both popped and unpopped).
- Provide containers labeled "popped" and "unpopped."
- Reproduce the instructions on page 51.

Materials in center:
- a container of unpopped corn kernels
- a container of 10 or more kernels of popped corn
- a ruler
- a balance scale
- instruction sheet

Prior Knowledge

1. Students need to understand these words:

popped	unpopped	kernels
measure	weigh	row
scale	estimate	handful

2. Students need to understand how to use a ruler and a balance scale.

3. Students need to have had experience with subtracting numbers and with estimation.

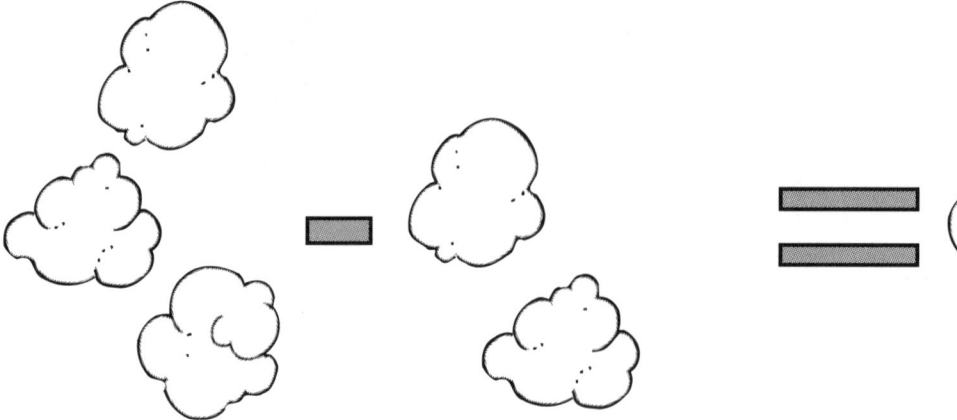

Popcorn Problems

_____   _____
name   date

Read all of the instructions.
Do the steps one at a time.

1. Put 10 unpopped kernels in a row.
   Measure the row.

   The row of unpopped kernels is _____ long.

2. Put 10 popped kernels in a row.
   Measure the row.

   The row of popped kernels is _____ long.

   How much longer is the row of popped kernels? _____

3. How many unpopped kernels does it take to make a row as long as 10 popped kernels?

   It takes _____ unpopped kernels.

4. Put 10 kernels of unpopped corn on one side of the scale.
   Put 10 kernels of popped corn on the other side of the scale.

   Which weighs the most? _____

5. Take a handful of unpopped kernels.
   Estimate how many kernels are in your hand.

   I think I have _____ kernels.

6. Count the handful of kernels.
   How many do you have?

   I have _____ kernels.

7. Do you have more or less kernels than your estimate?

   I have _____ kernels. How many? _____
   (more - less)

©1997 by Evan-Moor   51   Reading to Follow Instructions EMC 567

Mix It Up
Reading Instructions at a Center

This center provides practice in reading instructions to complete an experiment.

Teacher Preparation

What to do:
- Bring in a supply of vinegar, water, and baking soda.
- Label each container according to its contents.
- Reproduce the instructions on page 53.

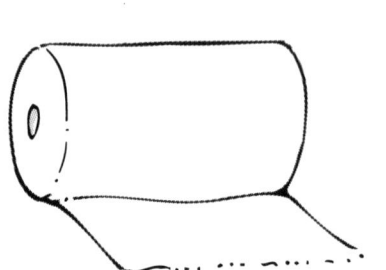

Materials in center:
- 2 plastic glasses
- a large spoon
- vinegar
- baking soda
- water
- paper towels (for spills)
- instruction sheet

Prior Knowledge

1. Students need to understand these words:

experiment	vinegar	baking soda
glass	fill	large
spoonful	water	question

2. Students need to understand how to write a description of what they observe.

3. Students need to know what 1/4 means.

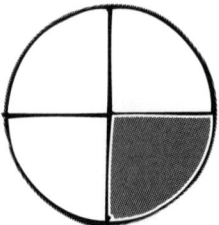

©1997 by Evan-Moor · 52 · Reading to Follow Instructions EMC 567

Mix It Up!

_____   _____
name   date

Read all of the instructions.
Do the steps one at a time.

> Question: What do you think will happen when you add baking soda to vinegar?
> _____
> _____

1. Fill one glass 1/4 full of vinegar.

2. Add 1 large spoonful of baking soda to the vinegar. Watch what happens.

3. Write what you see.   Draw what you see.

4. Now do the experiment again. Use water instead of vinegar.

5. Write what you see.   Draw what you see.

6. Clean up your work area.

©1997 by Evan-Moor   Reading to Follow Instructions EMC 567

Bird in a Cage
Reading Instructions at a Center

This center provides practice in reading instructions to make something.

Teacher Preparation

What to do:
- Provide plastic straws without a bendable joint.
- Make a 4" square (10 cm) template out of cardboard.
- Put out tagboard scraps (pieces must be larger than 4" (10 cm) squares).
- Reproduce the instructions on page 55.

Materials in center:
- template
- tagboard
- scissors
- felt-tip pens
- glue
- instruction sheet

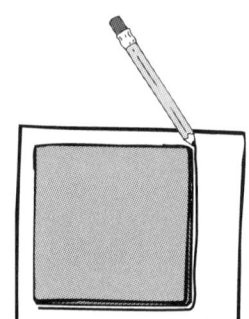

Prior Knowledge

1. Students need to understand these words:

trace	square	tagboard
template	birdcage	other side
straw	dry	between

2. Students need to know how to use a template.

3. Students need to know what a birdcage looks like.

©1997 by Evan-Moor — Reading to Follow Instructions EMC 567

Bird in a Cage

_____ _____
name   date

Read all of the instructions.
Do the steps one at a time.

1. Lay the template on the tagboard.
   Trace the square.

2. Cut out the square.

3. Draw a birdcage on one side of the tagboard.

4. Draw a small bird on the other side.
   Make the bird in the center of the square.

5. Make an X on the tagboard under the birdcage.

6. Put a drop of glue on the X.
   Lay the end of the straw on the glue.
   Let the glue dry.

7. Spin the straw between your hands.
   Can you see the bird in its cage?

©1997 by Evan-Moor

Stones in a Bowl Game
Reading Instructions at a Center

This center contains a game played by many Native American tribes. Fruit pits were used as playing pieces. In this version, students will use small, somewhat flat rocks.

Teacher Preparation

What to do:
- Collect small, flattish stones. Paint one side of the stones black. Leave the other side the natural color.
- Provide a small wooden bowl.
- Place 20 lima beans in a small box labeled "counters."
- Reproduce the instructions on page 57.

Materials in center:
- 6 stones
- a small wooden bowl
- 20 lima beans for counters
- instruction sheet

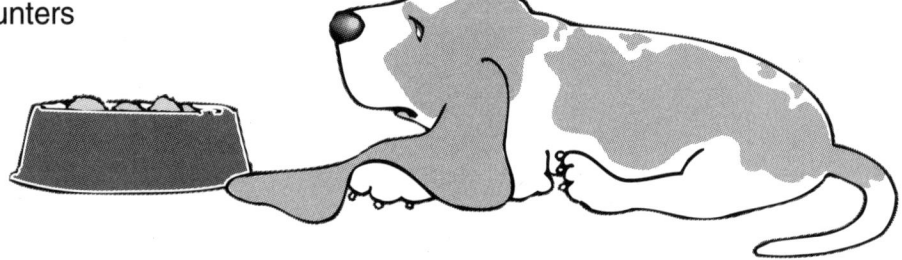

Prior Knowledge

1. Students need to understand these words:

stones	counters	facing
bowl	floor	score
point	player	bounce

2. Students will need to know how to tap the bowl on the floor to make the stones jump up and turn over.

3. Each player taps the bowl on the floor. The player with the greatest number of black sides up goes first.

Stones in a Bowl Game

Read all of the instructions.
Do the steps one at a time.

Get Ready

1. This is a game for two players.
   Sit on the floor.
   Put the bowl between you.

2. Each player gets 10 counters.

3. Put the six stones in the bowl.

4. Pick who gets to be first.

Play the Game

1. The player taps the bowl on the floor to make the stones jump.

2. Sit the bowl on the floor.
   Look at the stones.
   See how many counters you get to take.

3. Give the bowl to the other player.

4. Take turns until one player has all of the counters.

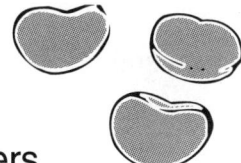

Scoring

If you see this, take 1 counter from the other player.

If you see this, take 5 counters from the other player.

If you see this, take 1 counter from the other player.

If you see this, take 5 counters from the other player.

If you see anything else, there is no score.

Write a Riddle
Reading Instructions at a Center

This center provides practice in reading instructions that explain how to write something.

Teacher Preparation

What to do:
- Cut pictures from magazines or reproduce those on pages 60 and 61. Cut the cards apart and place them in a folder or a small box.
- Reproduce the instructions on page 59.

Materials in center:
- picture cards
- pens and pencils
- paste or glue
- instruction sheet

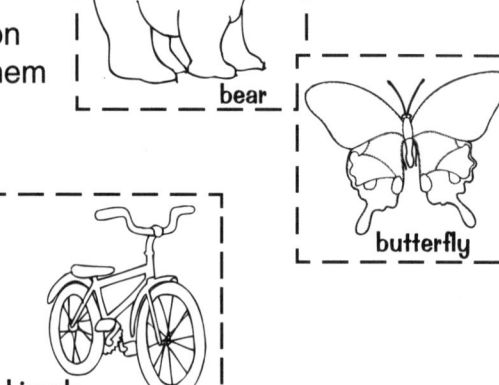

Prior Knowledge

1. Students need to understand these words:

riddle	clue
picture	sound
object	

2. Students need to understand what makes something a riddle. (Riddles give clues and ask questions.)

3. Students need to know words to describe an object, its sound (adjectives), and its actions (verbs).

Write a Riddle

Read all of the instructions.
Do the steps one at a time.

1. Pick a picture.

2. Think about the object in the picture.

   What does it look like?
   What can it do?
   What sound does it make?

3. Write a riddle on the lines below.
   Give clues that describe the object.
   Don't give away the object's name.

4. Cut on the dotted line.
   Fold it on the line.

5. Paste the picture inside.

I am: _____

what it looks like

I can: _____

what it can do

I make this sound : _____

what sound it makes

fold | What am I?

Note: Reproduce these cards to use in the *Write a Riddle* center.

Note: Reproduce these cards to use in the *Write a Riddle* center.

A Flying Machine
Reading Instructions at a Center

Students follow instructions to put together a "flying machine." The activity is extended by having them "pilot" the flying machine outdoors. They try to determine the best throwing technique to get it to glide the greatest distance. and they try to get it to make a loop in the air.

Teacher Preparation

What to do:
- Provide plastic straws without a bendable joint.
- Reproduce the flying machine pieces on page 64.
- Reproduce the instructions on page 63.

Materials in center:
- scissors
- tape
- measuring tape or yard stick
- crayons or marking pens
- flying machine pieces
- instruction sheet
- plastic straws

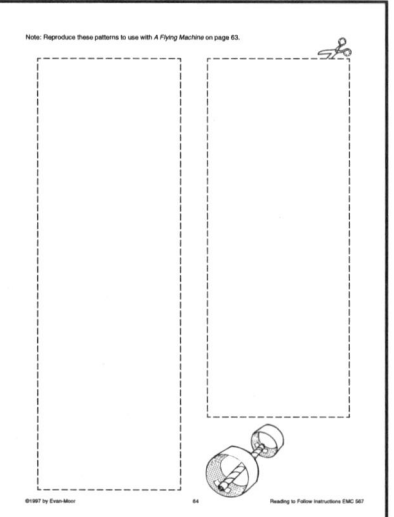

Prior Knowledge

1. Students need to understand these words:

design	colorful	straight
strip	ring	loops
overlap	parts	permission

2. Students need to know how to use tape to make rings and to attach objects to a straw.

3. Students need to know how to use a measuring instrument (tape, yardstick) to measure distance.

©1997 by Evan-Moor   62   Reading to Follow Instructions EMC 567

A Flying Machine

Read all of the instructions.
Do the steps one at a time.

1. Make a colorful design on the flying machine parts.

2. Cut out the flying machine parts.

3. Overlap the long strip.
   Tape the ends together.

4. Overlap the short strip.
   Tape the ends together.

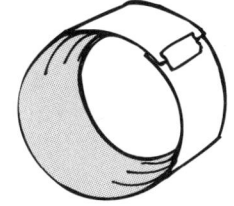

5. Tape the big ring to one end of the straw.

6. Tape the small ring to the other end of the straw.

7. Go outside. (Get permission from your teacher first.)
   Take a yardstick or measuring tape with you.
   Throw your flying machine into the air.

8. Answer these questions:
   _____
   _ _ _ _ _ _ _ _ _ _ _ _

   Did it go straight? _____
   _____
   _ _ _ _ _ _ _ _ _ _ _ _

   Did it make any loops? _____
   _____
   _ _ _ _ _ _ _ _ _ _ _ _

   How far did it go? _____
   _____
   _ _ _ _ _ _ _ _ _ _ _ _
   _____

Note: Reproduce these patterns to use with *A Flying Machine* on page 63.